Erstes Englisch mit Billy Malone

Vokabelquiz

At school

Lernen

TESSLOFF

Willkommen bei den Malones!

Mary

Peter

Charly

Sally

Billy

Susan

What do you call a child who goes to school?

Wie nennt man ein Kind, das zur Schule geht?

1. pupil

2. brother

3. sister

The right answer is:

Die richtige Antwort ist:

1. pupil
Schüler

pupil ['pju:pl] – Schüler
brother ['brʌðə] – Bruder
sister ['sɪstə] – Schwester

Who gives the pupils lessons?

Wer unterrichtet die Schüler?

1. baker

2. teacher

3. chef

The right answer is:

Die richtige Antwort ist:

2. teacher
Lehrer

baker ['beɪkə] – Bäcker
teacher ['tiːʧə] – Lehrer
chef [ʃef] – Koch

Where does the teacher normally sit?

Wo sitzt der Lehrer normalerweise?

1. on the cupboard

2. on the floor

3. at the desk

The right answer is:

Die richtige Antwort ist:

3. at the desk
am Pult

on the cupboard – auf dem Schrank
[ɒn ðə 'kʌbəd]
on the floor [ɒn ðə 'flɔː] – auf dem Boden
at the desk [æt ðə 'desk] – am Pult

What do you call this?

Wie nennt man diesen Gegenstand?

1. map

2. satchel

3. pencil case

The right answer is:

Die richtige Antwort ist:

2. satchel
Schultasche

map [mæp] – Landkarte
satchel ['sætʃl] – Schultasche
pencil case ['pensl,keɪs] – Federmäppchen

Where is the pencil case?

Wo liegt das Federmäppchen?

1. in the satchel

2. under the satchel

3. behind the satchel

The right answer is:

Die richtige Antwort ist:

3. behind the satchel
hinter der Schultasche

in [ɪn] – in
under ['ʌndə] – unter
behind [bɪ'haɪnd] – hinter

What is hanging on the wall?

Was hängt an der Wand?

1. map

2. book

3. rubber

The right answer is:

Die richtige Antwort ist:

1. map
Landkarte

map [mæp] – Landkarte
book [bʊk] – Buch
rubber ['rʌbə] – Radiergummi

What is Billy wearing?

Was hat Billy an?

1. pyjamas

2. school uniform

3. shorts

The right answer is:

Die richtige Antwort ist:

2. school uniform
Schuluniform

pyjamas [pɪ'dʒɑːməz] – Schlafanzug
school uniform – Schuluniform
[ˌskuːl 'juːnɪfɔːm]
shorts [ʃɔːts] – kurze Hose

Where is the teacher standing?

Wo steht die Lehrerin?

1. at the window

2. at the door

3. at the blackboard

The right answer is:

Die richtige Antwort ist:

3. at the blackboard
an der Tafel

window ['wɪndəʊ] – Fenster
door [dɔː] – Tür
blackboard ['blækbɔːd] – Tafel

What do you use to write on the blackboard?

Womit schreibt man auf die Tafel?

1. biro

2. chalk

3. pencil

The right answer is:

Die richtige Antwort ist:

2. chalk
Kreide

biro ['baɪərəʊ] – Kugelschreiber
chalk [tʃɔːk] – Kreide
pencil ['pensl] – Bleistift

What colour is Sally's school uniform?

Welche Farbe hat Sallys Schuluniform?

1. blue

2. yellow

3. brown

The right answer is:

Die richtige Antwort ist:

1. blue
blau

blue [bluː] – blau
yellow ['jeləʊ] – gelb
brown [braʊn] – braun

How many pencils are lying on the desk?

Wie viele Bleistifte liegen auf dem Pult?

1. twelve

2. five

3. eight

The right answer is:

Die richtige Antwort ist:

2. five
fünf

twelve [twelv] – zwölf
five [faɪv] – fünf
eight [eɪt] – acht

What subject is Mr Burt teaching?

Welches Fach unterrichtet Herr Burt gerade?

1. reading

2. music

3. maths

The right answer is:

Die richtige Antwort ist:

3. maths
Mathematik

reading ['riːdɪŋ] – Lesen
music ['mjuːzɪk] – Musik
maths [mæθs] – Mathematik

Where do you write your homework down?

Wohin schreibst du deine Hausaufgaben?

1. exercise book
2. atlas
3. timetable

The right answer is:

Die richtige Antwort ist:

1. exercise book
Heft

exercise book ['eksəsaɪzˌbʊk] – Heft
atlas ['ætləs] – Atlas
timetable ['taɪmˌteɪbl] – Stundenplan

In which subject do you learn to draw?

In welchem Fach lernt man Zeichnen?

1. science

2. art

3. physical education

The right answer is:

Die richtige Antwort ist:

2. art
Kunst

science [saɪəns] – Naturwissenschaft
art [ɑːt] – Kunst
physical education – Sport
[ˌfɪzɪkl edʒʊ'keɪʃn]

Which colour is the exercise book on top?

Welche Farbe hat das oberste Heft?

1. pink

2. black

3. green

The right answer is:

Die richtige Antwort ist:

3. green
grün

pink [pɪŋk] – rosa
black [blæk] – schwarz
green [griːn] – grün

What does the teacher normally write on?

Worauf schreibt der Lehrer normalerweise?

1. wall

2. blackboard

3. door

The right answer is:

Die richtige Antwort ist:

2. blackboard
Tafel

wall [wɔːl] – Wand
blackboard [ˈblækbɔːd] – Tafel
door [dɔː] – Tür

What do you write with in your exercise book?

Womit schreibst du in dein Heft?

1. pen

2. sponge

3. paintbox

The right answer is:

Die richtige Antwort ist:

1. pen
Füller

pen [pen] – Füller
sponge [spʌnʤ] – Schwamm
paintbox ['peɪntbɒks] – Malkasten

Which subject is Billy getting ready for?

Auf welches Fach bereitet sich Billy gerade vor?

1. religious education

2. maths

3. physical education

The right answer is:

Die richtige Antwort ist:

3. physical education
Sport

religious education – Religion
[rɪˌlɪʤəs eʤʊ'keɪʃn]
maths [mæθs] – Mathematik
physical education – Sport
[ˌfɪzɪkl eʤʊ'keɪʃn]

What do you call these?

Wie nennt man diese Stifte?

1. felt-tip pens

2. crayons

3. pencils

The right answer is:

Die richtige Antwort ist:

2. crayons
Buntstifte

felt-tip pen [ˌfelttɪp 'pen] – Filzstift
crayon ['kreɪɒn] – Buntstift
pencil ['pensl] – Bleistift

In which subject do you learn about animals?

In welchem Fach lernt man etwas über Tiere?

1. general studies

2. English

3. music

The right answer is:

Die richtige Antwort ist:

1. general studies
Sachkunde

general studies – Sachkunde
[ˌʤenrl 'stʌdiz]
English ['ɪŋglɪʃ] – Englisch
music ['mjuːzɪk] – Musik

What do you call this?

Wie nennt man diesen Gegenstand?

1. pencil case

2. exercise book

3. blackboard

The right answer is:

Die richtige Antwort ist:

1. pencil case
Federmäppchen

pencil case – Federmäppchen
['pensl,keɪs]
exercise book ['eksəsaɪz,bʊk] – Heft
blackboard ['blækbɔːd] – Tafel

What can you eat during break-time?

Was kann man in der Pause essen?

1. crayons

2. apple

3. ruler

The right answer is:

Die richtige Antwort ist:

2. apple
Apfel

crayon ['kreɪɒn] – Buntstift
apple ['æpl] – Apfel
ruler ['ruːlə] – Lineal

How many crayons are there in the pencil case?

Wie viele Buntstifte sind im Federmäppchen?

1. two

2. six

3. nine

The right answer is:

Die richtige Antwort ist:

2. six
sechs

two [tuː] – zwei
six [sɪks] – sechs
nine [naɪn] – neun

Where is Billy sitting?

Wo sitzt Billy gerade?

1. on the chair

2. on the floor

3. on the desk

The right answer is:

Die richtige Antwort ist:

1. on the chair
auf dem Stuhl

chair [ʧeə] – Stuhl
floor [flɔː] – Fußboden
desk [desk] – Pult

What subject is Mrs Smith teaching?

Welches Fach unterrichtet Frau Smith gerade?

1. English

2. French

3. German

The right answer is:

Die richtige Antwort ist:

3. German
Deutsch

English ['ɪŋglɪʃ] – Englisch
French [frenʃ] – Französisch
German ['ʤɜːmən] – Deutsch

How many books are in Billy's satchel?

Wie viele Bücher sind in Billys Schultasche?

1. three

2. eleven

3. four

The right answer is:

Die richtige Antwort ist:

1. three
drei

three [θriː] – drei
eleven [ɪ'levn] – elf
four [fɔː] – vier

What kind of sport is Billy doing?

Welchen Sport macht Billy gerade?

1. swimming

2. gymnastics

3. basketball

The right answer is:

Die richtige Antwort ist:

2. gymnastics
Turnen

swimming ['swɪmɪŋ] – Schwimmen
gymnastics [dʒɪm'næstɪks] – Turnen
basketball ['baːskɪtbɔːl] – Basketball

What do you learn in physical education?

Was lernt man im Sport-unterricht?

1. to play cards

2. to play football

3. to play the piano

The right answer is:

Die richtige Antwort ist:

2. to play football
Fußball spielen

cards [kɑːdz] – Karten
football ['fʊtbɔːl] – Fußball
piano [pi'ænəʊ] – Klavier

At what time can you eat, drink and talk?

Wann kannst du essen, trinken und dich unterhalten?

1. during class

2. during break-time

3. during art lessons

The right answer is:

Die richtige Antwort ist:

2. during break-time
während der Pause

class [klaːs] – Unterricht
break-time ['breɪktaɪm] – Pause
art lesson ['aːt ˌlesn] – Kunststunde

Where is the lunch-box?

Wo liegt die Brotzeitbox?

1. in front of the satchel

2. next to the satchel

3. on top of the satchel

The right answer is:

Die richtige Antwort ist:

3. on top of the satchel
auf der Schultasche

in front of [ɪn 'frʌnt əv] – vor
next to ['nekst tuː] – neben
on top of [ɒn 'tɒp əv] – auf

How many sweets is Billy trading for a crayon?

Wie viele Gummibärchen tauscht Billy für einen Stift?

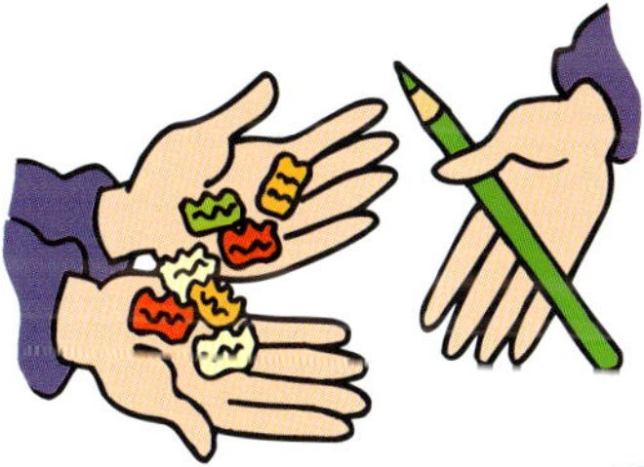

1. seven

2. ten

3. one

The right answer is:

Die richtige Antwort ist:

1. seven
sieben

seven ['sevn] – sieben
ten [ten] – zehn
one [wʌn] – eins

What is Mr Burt writing on the blackboard?

Was schreibt Herr Burt an die Tafel?

1. words

2. letters

3. numbers

The right answer is:

Die richtige Antwort ist:

3. numbers
Zahlen

word [wɜːd] – Wort
letter ['letə] – Buchstabe
number ['nʌmbə] – Zahl

What do you normally find in a pencil case?

Was findet man normalerweise im Federmäppchen?

1. ruler

2. book

3. sweets

The right answer is:

Die richtige Antwort ist:

1. ruler
Lineal

ruler ['ruːlə] – Lineal
book [bʊk] – Buch
sweets [swiːts] – Süßigkeiten

Where is Sally sitting?

Wo sitzt Sally?

1. behind Billy

2. on Billy's left

3. in front of Billy

The right answer is:

Die richtige Antwort ist:

1. behind Billy
hinter Billy

behind [bɪ'haɪnd] – hinter
on ... left [ɒn ... 'left] – links von
in front of [ɪn 'frʌnt əv] – vor

What is Billy painting with?

Womit malt Billy gerade?

1. crayon

2. paintbrush

3. chalk

The right answer is:

Die richtige Antwort ist:

2. paintbrush
Pinsel

crayon ['kreɪɒn] – Buntstift
paintbrush ['peɪntbrʌʃ] – Pinsel
chalk [ʧɔːk] – Kreide

What do you clean the blackboard with?

Womit wischt man die Tafel?

1. sponge

2. rubber

3. bag

The right answer is:

Die richtige Antwort ist:

1. sponge
Schwamm

sponge [spʌndʒ] – Schwamm
rubber ['rʌbə] – Radiergummi
bag [bæg] – Tasche

What colour is the satchel?

Welche Farbe hat die Schultasche?

1. red

2. white

3. purple

The right answer is:

Die richtige Antwort ist:

1. red
rot

red [red] – rot
white [waɪt] – weiß
purple ['pɜːpl] – lila

What do you need for your sports lesson?

Was braucht man für den Sportunterricht?

1. trainers

2. paintbox

3. map

The right answer is:

Die richtige Antwort ist:

1. trainers
Turnschuhe

trainers ['treɪnəz] – Turnschuhe
paintbox ['peɪntbɒks] – Malkasten
map [mæp] – Landkarte

Vokabelquiz

Quadratisch – englisch – gut

In der Reihe Vokabelquiz sind folgende Titel erschienen:

ISBN 978-3-7886-1578-9

ISBN 978-3-7886-1581-9

ISBN 978-3-7886-1582-6

ISBN 978-3-7886-1579-6

ISBN 978-3-7886-1580-2

SBN 978-3-7886-1583-3

Von Manfred Tophoven durchgehend farbig illustriert. Ab 3. Klasse. **Je €[D] 4,80**